FROM THE LIPS OF
THE GODDESS

FROM THE LIPS
OF
THE GODDESS

Mata Vaishno Devi

Rajesh Talwar

Publications
KALPAZ PUBLICATIONS
DELHI-110052

FROM THE LIPS OF THE GODDESS
Mata Vaishno Devi

Rs. 90

ISBN : 81-7835-590-6

© Rajesh Talwar

Published in 2006 in India by
Kalpaz Publications
C-30, Satyawati Nagar, Delhi-110052
E-mail : kalaz@hotmail.com

Laser Type-setting by: Shagun Graphics, Delhi
Printed At: Salasar Imaging System, Delhi

For
ROOPALI

Contents

Introduction

The idea of writing this book came to me last September when after five years of traveling and working in different parts of the world I returned to base in NOIDA, near New Delhi and soon thereafter embarked on a trip to Mata Vaishno Devi.

One of the things I realized after spending a great deal of time overseas was that India is in modern times uniquely positioned with respect to Goddesses. Mary, mother of Jesus commands similar reverence, but ultimately she is regarded by most Christians as the mother of God, and not a Goddess in her own right in the same way in which Durga, Lakshmi and Sarawati are worshipped in this country.

An African woman from Liberia was furious at my suggestion that God could be a woman! No, she said, it's an outrageous suggestion! God most certainly is a MAN. In India though God is many things: man, woman and sometimes a combination of man and woman or even man and animal!

In the world today it is also only in India that we have so many Goddesses, be they river Goddesses like Ganga Maiya or Goddesses of Wealth (Lakshmi), of Learning (Sarawati) or of Power (Shakti or Durga). Social anthropologists, who can be too rational, may argue that it is a historical aberration that continues in the modern age and there is really nothing very special about the Indian belief system because the Romans too had their Goddesses as had the Greeks. I am no scholar but I do know that the mindset of the people who worshipped those Goddesses in Europe in centuries gone by is completely different from that in India. No, when I say *completely* different I must accept that I use exaggerated phraseology. Truly speaking, there are many amongst us whose worship of the Indian Goddesses **can** be compared to the attitude of the Greeks or the Romans, but yet they are not truly representative of the Indian spirit.

Can you imagine for a moment what it would mean if Londoners were to worship the Thames or Europeans the Danube as a Goddess descended from heaven? It seems laughable but I for one do not envy them their supra rationality which is just another term for lack of vision or discernment. They are perhaps more aware today than the Indians are of the environmental crisis that faces our planet but their world view which essentially regarded nature as something to be conquered by man could not have thought of nature and its varied manifestations as possessing a sacred or holy character. The worship of rivers in Europe is a laughable idea as it would require a completely different mind set, a completely different world view and one that essentially positions Nature as being outside Godliness. But this is not a book about the worship of Ganga Maiya though that too is a book that can and will be written one day, but a book about the worship of perhaps the most revered Goddess in North India.

It is a strange irony that sometimes I feel that more and more people in India are worshipping Gods and Goddesses in the Greek fashion and in a strange reversal in modern times people are reverting back to worshipping the Goddess as it was done by the Greeks and the Romans. Please note the distinction. I am not saying that worshipping Goddesses is ancient. I am saying that the worship of Goddesses today is being done in an ancient way, and in earlier centuries, the ancient Indians worshipped Goddesses in a much more modern spirit. (I am using modern here to convey the notion of sophistication as opposed to primitiveness.) The reason for this is consumerism, greed and the vast array of objects of desire that surround us in our shopping malls. I am no socialist but I do believe in the self containment of human greed and avarice and I fear that increasingly many of us who go to worship at the altar of the Goddess go there motivated by relatively primitive notions of rewards and benefits. I repeat, there is nothing wrong in seeking wealth, but I do feel we are somewhere becoming more primitive in our attitudes.

When the idea of writing down my experiences into book form first came to me I was initially hesitant. What credibility did I command for writing a book on the Goddess? I was no famed Indologist, no acclaimed researcher at the School of Oriental and African Studies and not even some one who had visited all the major religious sites in India. But as soon as the thought came to me, it was replaced by another thought. If there was anything at all to this experience Mata would find a way.

I had grown up hearing stories of the Devi from my grandmother but I heard them less in a religious

spirit and more as a child who is fascinated with tales involving demons and monsters. In essential terms I heard them no differently from how I see today's kids read stories involving superheroes and supervillains in comic strips or watch them on television. However I now realize that while those mythological tales often had a hidden message that would become apparent only much later, the stories that today's generation are being acquainted with possess no such higher meaning.

According to Vedic scholars there are four Purusharth or objectives of a human life. There is Dharm (Righteousness), Arth (Material Pursuits), Kaam (Contentment) and Moksh (Enlightenment). The Goddess Mata Vaishno Devi is believed to grant all the four boons to those who visit Her Holy Shrine. She is considered to fulfill anything and everything that a person wishes for in life, *in a righteous way*. Many of us who go for the pilgrimage to Her shrine forget the existence of that caveat and indeed I too realized for the first time what those words 'in a righteous way' meant when I had Her *darshan*.

During my trip to Mata Vaishno Devi last September, at the time of my *darshan*, I experienced a strange phenomenon which I will recount here. I felt the Goddess speak to me directly. Her voice was human and at the same time not human. When I say not human I mean only to say that it had purity that one never comes across in this life.

Mata spoke to me and at the same time She spoke to the seven other people who were gathered before Her shrine. Our *darshan* could not have lasted more than five minutes for we were hurried along so that the others who were waiting in the queue behind us could have their *darshan*.

When the Goddess spoke to me, I heard Her speak clearly but at the same time through some miracle I heard Her speak to all the others who were gathered in the cave. I heard Her speak to them at the same time as She spoke to me and yet what She said was completely different even though there was a unifying thread behind each word that She uttered. Her voice was like a musical symphony in which you can hear each individual instrument and yet hear the whole music all at once. I heard more clearly than I have ever heard anything in my life and my fellow travelers tell me that I had to sit down on the floor and appeared to be in a dazed - or dare I say momentarily awakened – state for approximately one minute.

A minute may seem too short, but even a minute can seem like an eternity if it is full of radiance. We lead shadowy lives for the most part of our stay on this earth and years pass away like days and days like hours even though paradoxically we find it more difficult to pass time.

Rationalists will of course say that all this business of hearing the Goddess speak to eight persons at the same time is just nonsense. They will judge my experience to have been hallucinatory. The more tolerant amongst them will say that I must have been suffering from a case of an overactive imagination. This may be so, and I would have no way of rebutting such a statement had it not been for the fact that after I awoke from that one minute of total silence I did recall what the Goddess spoke to each one of us.

There are some who have read the foregoing pages and told me how the words resonated in their hearts but there have also been some who have said that these are invented lies. It may be that the words have not struck a chord in their hearts because I have not been able to accurately describe the event or perhaps I was not hollowed enough as a medium or flute for the music to pour through me (for the words of the Mother are nothing if not celestial music) or it may be that they are still stuck in science and logic, or to take a still less charitable explanation it may also be that they are jealous and angry.

It was the Goddess who spoke and there was very little said by any of us who had gathered to receive Her *darshan*, with the exception perhaps of young Parwati, the prostitute from Jammu. This is a measure perhaps of the Mata's benevolence for after we had heard her I realized how she more than anyone else in our group needed to speak and to be heard.

But I will not take any more of your time. Here, hear it yourself. From the lips of the Goddess.

R.T.

August 15, 2006

Chapter 1

The Darshan

AS THE GROUP SLOWLY MADE ITS WAY towards the shrine that they had now almost reached a strange exultation seized S.

The tiredness slipped away from his body and he was even unmindful anymore of the wet and cold carpet that had so chilled his naked feet during the last phase of the journey. The pilgrimage was finally coming to an end and he would finally be face to face with the Goddess.

They were a group of eight and amongst them was a merchant, a childless couple seeking the boon of a child, an aged man, a scientist, a prostitute, an artist, and finally there was S himself, the seeker.

They were there inside the cave only for a few minutes but the Goddess spake to them for long. S glimpsed the poet's vision of seeing eternity in a moment, for it was the strangest of all *darshans* that he had had, lasting a few moments and at the same time having the depth of intimacy that only the knowledge of his past lives could have brought to someone.

The Goddess spoke to him and simultaneously She addressed all the others who had gathered there. But first She addressed all of them as a group.

MY CHILDREN, (she said), YOU HAVE come to your mother and will not go back empty handed. You may not get what you wanted, for it does not behove the true mother to always give to her children what they want but rather to give them what they want and *what they truly need* and quite often the two of them are poles apart for the child seeks only to satisfy his taste buds but the mother seeks to provide him with real nourishment which too shall not be without taste if he has only the patience to savor it.

There are hundreds of thousands of devotees who have come to me over the centuries and hundreds of thousands more who are coming and will keep coming.

Why then do they come to me instead of going elsewhere to so many of the other Gods, who are no less powerful? You do not see such a rush at their temples and neither do you see such a frenzy of chanting there. Yet they come to me shouting, 'Jai Mata Di'. And again they shout, 'Jai Mata Di.' And repeat the same endlessly without tiring.

There are children who go to their father to ask for something and then when they are refused they go to the mother in the hope that she will not refuse them or even that she will exert her influence over the father to give them what they desire.

Those who come to me are often like those self same children who have grown in years, sprouted beards and moustaches, but internally they remain the same little child who had more faith that the mother will give them what his little heart desires.

They come to the mother because they are afraid that the father will ask them sternly what they have been doing with their lives. They will be closely questioned on their past conduct and will have to give assurances of being on their best behavior in the future and even then there are no guarantees that they will get what they want.

'So what is the point?' they ask themselves. Better by far to go to the mother who will be so happy to see her child (though she may feign anger) even if he has muddied himself in the playground, even if he has fought with his play mates and even if has committed SINS. For many amongst you feel that you are not worthy of being in the presence of the father but the mother will accept you as you are, warts and all.

You come to me also because you can share your secret longings with me. The boy can tell his mother that he wants a doll should he desire one but will be fearful of disclosing this to the father for fear of ridicule. And it is not only the case with boys for girls too can say many things to their mother which they would deign not to say to their father.

Your relationship with me is more intimate as well apart from being more loving and therefore you have come to me, my children. You have come to the Mother Goddess.

And there are those amongst you who have come to ask for a mannat (wish to be fulfilled) and it is said that when you come to ask for a mannat you should not disclose it to anyone, even to he who is closest to you, for the asking of the mannat is an intimate secret between the child and the mother.

And when you come to me it is not only an intimate secret but it becomes an intimate and SACRED secret between you and me. And then if and when your mannat is granted, you are required to make in good time a repeat visit to the shrine to say your thanks.

There is something unique about some of the devotees who come to me. They say they felt a compulsion to move here for the *darshan*. Explaining what are sometimes sudden overnight departures to the shrine they say to others, 'Mata ka bulawa aya hai' and when they say this they say so in all sincerity and do not do so to claim for themselves any special merit or status.

Do I then call people? People sometimes who know little about me in text book terms yet people who have somehow sensed who I am and what I represent. Yes, I do call such people to have my *darshan* for I sense that they need to be close to their Mother for some time, not only to receive her love but to give theirs.

The Mother has called me, they say, and then they put aside all their work, all their commitment, all their petty and major concerns and they come to They come to me, they sing the songs in my praise, they tolerate the discomfort, they prostate themselves before my three images and then they fall at my feet and they cry. And they cry. And they cry. But they do not cry in sorrow. Or to put in more correctly, they do not cry only in sorrow. They cry in happiness, but it is a strange kind of happiness, rarely experienced in this world, for it is tinged with a sorrow. The sorrow is there for they have been away from me and the knowledge is uppermost in their minds that they will soon after the *darshan* be going away once again. When they are away it is not they forget me or that I forget them but other concerns then gather momentum, till the time comes once again that they feel they must have my *darshan* once again. These are the devotees who return to me time after time.

I could go on and on telling you why you have come to me, but you yourself know it inside why you have chosen to come here, and although I know that all the other Gods and Goddesses are above the petty envies and jealousies that plague lesser mortals (though often the mythologies concerning them would suggest otherwise) still let me not give any more examples of why you all come to me lest it appear that I am swelling in pride.

As the sages have long said in their wisdom: *'Pratyaksh ka pramand kya?'* In other words what is the need to give the proof or reasoning behind what is so self evident. You have come to the Mother and She will take care!

You have come to me as your Mother and as I have said you will not be turned away if you have come in all sincerity for it is well known that no one goes away empty handed from the shrine of the Mata.'

And then the Goddess paused in Her speech and S saw that that there was a garland before the central pindi (rock formation) to the shrine which had nine white flowers ringed through a thread that was now broken and it seemed that they had all either not noticed the garland before or that it had magically appeared.

And it seemed that the Goddess wished them to each take away a flower for they were magically drawn to the garland and they saw that the string holding the flowers together had come undone, and each of them, including S took away a flower and retreated a short distance to their former positions.

And S put the delicate white flower in his front short pocket so that it peeped out.

And then the Goddess continued to speak repeating Her last words to them:

'You have come to me as your Mother and as I have said you will not be turned away if you have come in all sincerity for it is well known that no one goes away empty handed from the shrine of the Mata

It is another matter that they may not know the value of what they carry back with them.'

Chapter 2

The Symbols

YOU KNOW ME AS THE MOTHER, Mata Vaishno Devi, and it is not a chance that my name is Vaishno Devi but I have this name because as a girl I was a devotee of Vishnu.

Brahma is the creator and Shiva is the destroyer, but I am chiefly the devotee of Vishnu for he preserves and is the force between the act of creation and destruction.

I am the ultimate creator as a Mother, for all births take place through the Mother but I am also a destroyer when I assume the form of Ma Kali or Durga whose energies have been poured into me, yet I am Vaishno Devi, the Mother who worships and symbolizes Vishnu who maintains and preserves for is that not the essential task of the Mother.

YOU HAVE SEEN ME so many times while awake and sometimes I have come to you in your dreams. You have seen me in my entire splendor, for although I am your Mother I am ever youthful. I did not spend many years in my earthly life and I am therefore young in terms of my physical living but I am also young in a deeper spiritual sense. I am young because you are all my children and children look to a youthful mother to help them in all their attempts at growing up. And thus whilst some of you might have crossed eighty years of this earthly existence you are for me still my children, who are trying hard to grow up.

When you see me, you see me resplendent in my attire but you see me also with certain weapons that are also symbols and are also decorative objects. You see me with the Trishul (trident) that was given me by Shiva, with the Sudharshan Chakra (constantly moving discus) that has been given to me by Vishnu and with the bow and arrows that were given to me by Vayu.

I shall not speak of the Trishul (even though I did use it to blast a hole through the cave at Garbha Joon and on numerous other occasions) or of the Sudharshan Chakra for you have heard of their powers from other sources and it is more appropriate

that you hear of their powers and meaning from
Shiva and Vishnu but let me tell you about the bows
and arrows of Agni, the lion from the Himalayas
and of the langurs who throng around me.

The Lion

You have read the stories about me, how I grant
wishes to those who come to my altar, and you have
seen me in all my finery, my hands on the bow and
arrow, one hand on my spear or trident and still
another on the chakra and I myself astride a lion.

So let me tell you today a bit more about the
meaning behind some of the symbols for those of you
who are less acquainted and there is only the rare
person amongst you who knows me well.

Why do you see me astride the lion? There are
some amongst you who believe that this shows my
power, but what power do lions have in the modern
world, where man has all but eliminated the species.
What power does the lion have compared to man
with all his weapons of destruction? Man too may
think that he has his feet on top of the lion and in
a sense this will be true, but when I have my feet on
top of the lion I am showing mastery not only over

the forces of nature but mastery over my inner being.

The lion roars in anger and all the beasts in the jungle are terrified and tamed. If you have control of that anger you are greater than the lion. I am not speaking in favor of timidity for I am saying have the lion inside you but keep it in absolute control – there is a profound difference between the two.

When the lion roars it resounds in far away mountains and valleys. When I have my feet on the lion it means that my message too resounds in far away mountains and valleys and even in that most far way place – your heart. If you do not hear the lions roar in your heart, it is not because I do not try to reach you but rather in spite of my trying to use even the lion's roar to grab your attention. Yet you do not listen!

I sit astride the lion. In some depictions he lies at my feet but that is because the lion is worthy of having my feet on him. He is at the feet of the Goddess, and so have you all come – to the feet of the Goddess, but you will truly be at my feet when I accept to treat you as a son, as a lion, as someone worthy. Hunters of prey put their feet on the object they capture which may be a crocodile, a tiger and in some instances even a lion. I have my feet on the lion for he is the king of the jungle, the largest member of the cat family and I want you too to be like lions. Be like lions and then when I place my feet on you, you too will gain mastery over your emotions.

I have spoken thus about the positive aspects of the lion, but the lion symbolizes other things as well and some of these are negative. The lion is a symbol of crudity. It is living in the lap of nature, but does it stop to watch beautiful sunsets or to make company with other animals. For the lion the other animals are just so much meat that will satisfy his hunger. And as I control the lion, the lion that is a symbol of crudity, so do I ask you to control all that is crude in you.

It is easy to mistake my meaning. I do not ask you to become vegetarians. I do not ask you to abstain from sex. And I do not even ask you to abandon crudity altogether. I do ask you to keep it subservient though to your higher nature and feelings. Eat your meat if you wish to but also watch the sunset and listen to the songs of the nightingale.

The Langur

Then you must have seen that I am always surrounded by langurs. Why do I surround myself with langurs, or rather why do I keep the company of monkeys? I do not seek their company but they come to me. But you will ask - Why are they drawn to me?

Many amongst you are langurs and you come to me pretending to be humans. You have the human form in this incarnation but inside you are pure monkey. Do not be offended by this. All species tend to have monkey elements in them. Do not they say that birds of a feather fly together? Well, not only do birds like to keep the company of other birds but they behave like each other. Man is special in this regard. He is a species but he has his own unique nature that is a Gift from above.

He should try to be true to his nature, but instead he is always looking around to copy what others are doing. And all others are also looking around to see what others are doing. Even when people come to pray to me, I see that they cast a look around to see how others are praying.

Be true to your nature. Do not be a langur. But if you come to me as a langur I will not turn you away because you have the potential and the fact that you have come to me makes you that little bit different from the other langurs who keep each others company but who have not had the vision to come to sit at the feet of the Goddess.

Bow and Arrows

You see me with my bow and arrows that have been given to me by the God Vayu, but these are not only for the purpose of killing the asuras (demons).

My arrows are aimed at you, at your heart. They seek to penetrate you so that you will make the effort to change. No one changes unless there is something propelling him. You too will not change without something pushing you from behind.

My arrows are always aimed at you, but you should be so lucky that they should hit you, for there is nothing grander than to be shot by an arrow from the quiver of the Goddess and if you die at her feet you will attain to the highest heaven that exists.

Chapter 3

The Legends

NOW THAT YOU HAVE UNDERSTOOD something about why I have chosen to appear in a certain form and with certain appendages that are my physical as well as spiritual symbols you need to know something concerning some of the major events of my earthly life. There are many stories and legends about me and not all of them are of equal importance.

My name is Vaishnavi which is given me because I have worshipped Vishnu, and Ram and Krishna are nothing if not avatars of Vishnu and therefore the story of my encounter with Lord Ram is one of the most important stories of my life.

But there are numerous other stories as well. In legends that concern many Gods and Goddesses there is often depicted the fight between good and evil and do you not see that fight everywhere today, not least within yourself.

The legends that you read or hear of can generally be appreciated by my devotees at two levels. They can enjoy the story at a literal level or at a higher metaphysical level where the stories are valuable not for a mere demonstration of my power but because they signify a higher meaning or truth.

Take for instance my encounter with the demon Mahishasura who was half man and half buffalo (born as a result of a union between Rambha and a she buffalo Mahishi). It is said that this was one of my most major and difficult battles and the story of how I vanquished the demon can enthrall my devotees. Children in particular are apt to listen wide eyed to such tales and it may be difficult to retain their attention otherwise. The stories thus do serve a purpose in having a literal meaning. However many amongst my disciples continue to remain like children by clinging to the literal meaning of the stories. They are not to be blamed for this.

There is however a higher meaning to some of the stories and those amongst you who are more mature should try to look for them. Ask yourself the question why Mahishasura the demon is so powerful. Why has the buffalo been chosen as a symbol instead of a tiger or a lion? And when you think hard you will yourself find the answer that perhaps it is the combination of a certain human intelligence with a buffalo like slothfulness and intransigence that is ruling much of the world today. It is this powerful combination that I set out to battle but having defeated it once it does not mean that it cannot rear its head again. You need to battle every time with the buffalo inside you even as you come to me for my *darshan*.

There are those amongst you who have come for my *darshan* who are akin to the langurs that crowd around me in my depictions and while you are imitators you carry little original sin inside you. It is just a manner of changing your direction, of making you recognize what lies inside you and then the langur will become my best disciple for he will then emulate rightly not only what he sees from outside (in a person who had connected with his inner being) but follow what he then recognizes to be within him.

My real battle though is with those who are half men and half a she buffalo. And even amongst my devotees there are both men and women who without realizing it are representatives of Mahishasura.

The God Agni decreed that Mahishasura would be so powerful that no male could defeat him and therefore it was up to me to slay him for which all the Gods are eternally grateful.

But today I am telling you that the battle is not over. Far from over. One of the most powerful asuras in the world today is still that self same Mahishasura, who is a combination of a man and a she buffalo. The buffalo represents utter and complete crudity, or in other words the total absence of any kind of refinement.

And there are those amongst you who come to me like that self same Mahishasura. You are my disciples and yet you are my worst enemy. It would be truer perhaps to say that you are yourself your worst enemy.

When I see the representatives of Mahishasura come to me with the langurs, I am thankful that there will be an opportunity for me to dent their armor and in the end to slay them. Not all the representatives of Mahishasura are alike for do not forget that in the ten thousand year battle that I waged against him before I finally chopped off his head, he came to me in the form of a buffalo, a lion, a man carrying a sword, an elephant and lastly again as a buffalo. It is not easy to kill a Mahishasura and he undergoes a strange transformation before he is finally slain.

Why did Agni say that Mahishasura could only be slain by a woman? Normally iron cuts iron, diamond cuts diamond, but Agni realized that this was one unique situation where crudity cannot be slain by crudity alone but by a crudity which still has an elegance and refinement about it, such that most Gods cannot command, but which I as the Goddess incarnate of three Mother Goddesses do possess in enough measure.

My meeting with Rama

They say that the power of the Devi knows no limits and it is also said that the stories about the power and grace of the Devi are endless.

There are so many stories about me and some of them do even contradict each other in some respects so that sometimes my devotees are at a loss, not knowing whom or what to believe.

Let me recount to you two of the better-known and important stories about my life even in case you have heard them already.

The first story concerns Ram. It is said there was a time when I had relinquished all earthly comforts and gone into the forest to meditate. During that period Ram too was in exile and he met me. When I saw him I at once recognized him as the incarnation of Lord Vishnu and wanted to be one with him. I asked him to merge me with him so that I could become one with the Supreme Creator. Lord Rama however felt it was not the appropriate time and dissuaded me. He promised though that he would visit me at the end of his exile and if at that time I succeeded in recognizing him he would grant me my wish.

It is said that Rama kept his promise to me and visited me at the end of his exile but at that time he came dressed as an old man and I failed to recognize him. Seeing me miserable and distraught at having failed to recognize him, Rama consoled me by telling me that the time had not yet come for me to merge myself with the Ultimate. It would happen though when during the time of Kalyug Rama reappeared as Kalki. Meanwhile he advised me to meditate and set up an Ashram at the base of the Trikuta hills.

It is said that I followed Rama's advice and once

I had set up my Ashram my fame spread far and wide and people flocked to see me and they have come ever since.

Now this is a well known story but like many of such stories there are two dimensions to it, the physical (or the factual) and the metaphysical which is the meaning of the story that is not always immediately apparent.

You come to me because I am your Mother, your Real Mother and your earthly mother is but a shadow of my real self.

And do you know why mothers are more indulgent to their children than fathers. It is because the mother loves the child so much that the child is almost a part of her being. She has her own psyche but she has also within her the psyche of her child, almost as if it were pasted onto her own psyche. The mother is the mother of the child but simultaneously she is the child herself, amazing as this may sound to you.

And until I lose that child inside me I will not attain to pure divinity.

I am divine. In fact it would be true to say that I am the essence of all divinity, for divinity is in its essence feminine energy and this you recognize when you come to me

At the same time Rama is not wrong when he said to me that I was not ready. I loved Rama and I wished to be united to him but he saw that as yet I was still too attached to the child such that I carry the child within me and THAT I WAS NOT PREPARED TO FORSAKE AND LEAVE THAT CHILD BEHIND

So it was a weary and amused Rama who said that I was not ready when he met me in the forest during the time of his exile. And he promised me that he would come again at the end of his exile to take me with him, should I then be ready.

And when he came, he came dressed as an OLD MAN. Do you know that of all disguises in the world why he should have taken the disguise of an old man?

It was symbolic. It was a test. It was as if to say, 'Think it over Mata. I have come to you in this guise as an Old Man only because you should fully understand that if you want to come with me you would have to leave your children behind. You have to look at my grey locks and beard and understand that you will no longer be with your children.

AND WHEN he came to me disguised as an old man, do you think that I truly failed to recognize him. I would have recognized him to be Ram anywhere and in any shape. Divinity cannot but fail to recognize another form of Divinity when it comes into its presence.

I recognized RAM but I did not go at once to him. I hesitated. I thought to myself. Can I live without my children? I will not only have to leave my children behind I will have to perform surgery on myself - and that too the most radical surgery ever known to man for I would have to tear a piece of my heart out of my heart and cast it away.

And when Rama saw that hesitation, he knew what was going on in my mind and not wanting to cause me further anguish he came up to me and said, 'Vaishnavi, I told you that I would come to you after my period of exile and I have come as I had promised, but...' and here he smiled, 'but you have failed to recognize me, have you not?' and seeing me mute he continued, 'and therefore I have to go away again not taking you with me.'

And he admonished me and said that he would come again during the time of Kalyug when he came as Kalki.

I have to go away one day, my child, for you see just as your psyche is fused with my psyche at the same time I am also fused with the beyond for I am divinity beyond all divinity.

I have to go away, you see, for while I am of this world yet I am no longer of this world.

But I will never abandon you.

Rather I will seek and try my best to take you with me.

Chapter 4

The Legend of Bhairon Nath

The story of Bhairon Nath

THERE IS A LEGEND CONCERNING ME that is often more misunderstood than understood and that is the legend concerning the killing of Bhairon Nath.

Many of my disciples come to me and they ask me as to why I permitted a temple for Bhairon Nath to be built at the site so close to my own shrine. They cannot stand that someone who should have disrespected the Mata should have a temple built in his honor so close to her shrine. Even if they accept that my forgiveness is all encompassing they cannot yet understand why I have said that after the disciple has had my *darshan* he will have the *darshan* of Bhairon Nath.

There are some amongst my disciples who are learned in the scriptures and they say that the Mata had ordained this because Bhairon Nath was himself a very learned man.

But there are my other disciples who are perhaps less learned but more emotionally attached to me and they cry vehemently that all learning is worthless and that the learning of Bhairon Nath cannot be respected because it was worth nothing in the end for he disrespected the Mata. There was one such disciple who as he prostrated himself before me even confessed that he had had visions of destroying the temple of Bhairon Nath.

I will today set to rest all these controversies. To the learned amongst my disciples I will have to say that you are wrong when you assume that I have permitted, even ordained that the temple of Bhairon Nath be built out of respect for his learning, and to those who are more emotional but less learned I will say that you too are wrong to be upset that a temple be built so close to my shrine of someone who disrespected me, for you mistake the true nature of the shrine. Today, I will explain all, but first let me repeat to you the legend for there may be some amongst you who have not heard of it.

It all happened at the time when I had begun my meditations and set up the Ashram at the saying of Rama. As Ramji had predicted people came even from far flung places spending many days in travel in large numbers for solace and to seek my blessings.

According to the legend a Tantrik named Gorakh Nath during one of his meditations chanced to have a vision of the original meeting between Lord Rama and me and he sent one of his disciples the self same Bhairon Nath to investigate whether I had indeed attained a higher spiritual status.

Bhairon Nath, it is said, became enamored of me. He wished to marry me despite my admonishments. At a bhandara (community meal) organized by Mata Sridhar the whole village was invited. Also invited was Guru Gorakh Nath along with his followers which included Bhairon Nath.

It is said that during the course of this bhandara Bhairon Nath persisted in his misbehavior and I ran towards to the mountains to continue my meditations in peace with Bhairon Nath following.

I broke journey at Banganga. I shot an arrow into the ground and water came out to quench my thirst with a drink of water and then continued upwards. I made some other stops and then finally when I reached the place where my shrine is presently located I assumed the form of Maha Kali and beheaded Bhairon Nath just outside the mouth of the cave. The severed head of Bhairon Nath fell with force at a distant hill top.

These are one set of facts and to someone who may have observed the events this could be the only true statement of events. But the truth lies elsewhere.

In truth, my children, Bhairon Nath symbolizes the essence of many of you who have come to visit me today.

I had set up my ashram and people were coming from far flung places as Lord Rama had predicted but we do not keep many years in our mortal frames and so I had decided long before the bhandara that the time had come when I should no longer be there as a physical presence but rather remain as a pure spiritual presence providing succor and relief to those who came to see me.

I had decided where I would have my shrine and it is not an accident that site I had chosen was at an elevation, for this is befitting of the abode of a

Goddess like me who contains the combined energies of Maha Kali, Maha Sarasvati and Maha Laxmi. It is also not an accident that you my devotees have to journey fourteen kilometers on foot before you get my *darshan*. But of these matters, I will speak a while later.

You see, children, painful as it is for me to say this and for you to hear this, Bhairon Nath symbolizes the manner in which many of you who will visit me today go about their business in the world today. You move in greed, in lust and without restraint or thought for what you are really doing and the result of your actions has therefore to inevitably be – DESTRUCTION. It was your severed head that fell off with such force on a hill top.

YOU WILL ASK HOW AND WHY?

You see Goddesses and Gods have only a limited time we can spend on the earth for the earthly body unlike the divine one is perishable. It exists for a limited time.

I wanted my work to continue long after I had left the earthly body and therefore I needed to choose my site, choose the occasion and choose also any events that may accompany my departure from the earthly life. And these choices would be made with but a single purpose in mind – your benefit.

So long before the bhandara had been organized I had been planning to say goodbye and to depart from my earthly form. When Bhairon Nath came to investigate me at the behest of his Guru, Guru Gorakh Nath it was in itself an improper act for Goddesses cannot be investigated in this fashion.

Anyhow I knew that he was observing me and I saw too that he did not give me the respect that he should have given me were he a true seeker of the truth. I repelled him but he was not dissuaded.

It was then that it occurred to me that might it not be a good idea for me to make an example of him on the occasion of my departure from this earthly life. I thought it would however be unfair of me not to give him an opportunity to repent and to follow the path of the true seeker for it is true that the Goddess is very merciful.

So it was that when my devotees organized the bhandara I finalized my plans with respect to my departure from this earthly life. I decided too that Bhairon Nath would be immortalized as a symbol of how despite all the learning that a man may have he can descend to the uncouth and even barbaric behavior sooner sometimes than the most unlettered peasant.

At the time of the bhandara together with the rest of the village Guru Gorakh Nath was also an invitee, and despite his presence his disciple Bhairon Nath continued his bad behavior. He was given every opportunity to repent and to ask for forgiveness but when he did not do so I decided that he would become a potent symbol that would assist the people who came henceforth to my shrine towards their spiritual destiny. You will ask, in what manner would this happen? I will explain.

Had I wanted to, I could have assumed the form of Maha Kali at the time of the bhandara itself in front of all the village gathering and in front of Guru Gorakh Nath himself and destroyed Bhairon Nath utterly, but I would have then have been unable to create a device for the spiritual transformation of those devotees who would thenceforth come to my shrine.

I pretended to escape and to seek refuge to carry out my further meditations but Bhairon Nath insisted on following me. I broke journey at Ban Ganga to quench my thirst and still he came after me. I made several stops afterwards and yet I saw he came after me.

I stopped at the cave at Adhkawari. I spent nine months there doing my meditation and this is the reason the cave is known as Garbh Joon. And it is true that I spent all this time in meditation for even at this stage I wished to give him an opportunity to repent. But there is another reason why I spent nine months there.

A mother takes nine months to bear a child into this world. The creative potential of a mother is fully realized only upon the expiry of nine months. And at the time, Goddess though I was, motherhood was my essential being and nature and even to attain to the beyond by virtue of my mother like nature, existence decreed that my creative potential and dissolution into the beyond, into the absolute could only be realized after nine months.

The first question is as to why I spent exactly nine months there inside the cave and the second question is why Bhairon Nath discovered me exactly after nine months. Was this purely coincidental?

No, it was not coincidental but by design.

As I said when a mother gives birth to a child it usually takes roughly nine months. What was I giving birth to in the cave that I took nine months? I was giving birth to myself. Rather I was sundering the portion that was tied to my children, for though I would continue to be closely connected to them from the spiritual world my connection to them in this material world was being severed and even that was immensely painful to me even though I had already decided that it would be the case. And so I spent nine months inside the cave at Adhkavari meditating and preparing myself for the physical separation from my children that would shortly ensue.

And when the nine months were over and I was truly ready to be reborn I allowed Bhairon Nath to discover me. There are those amongst my followers who believe that I was hiding from Bhairon Nath and yet they believe that I am All Powerful. I was not hiding from Bhairon Nath, although it is true that he was seeking me. When he came to the cave, did I not then blast a hole through the other side of the cave with my trident? And still he followed.

It is said that I spent nine months there but Bhairon Nath finally located me there and I blasted a hole in the other side of the cave with the Trident given to me by Shiva.

I left the cave at Adhkawari and finally reached the Holy Cave at Darbar, which is the place I had marked for my shrine. It was at that juncture that I decided that it would be an appropriate place to demonstrate my powers. At once I assumed the form of Maha Kali and severed Bhairon Nath's head.

And then I decreed (most amazingly to some of you) that there would be a temple in the name of Bhairon Nath and I also decreed that after the devotees had my *darshan* they would have a *darshan* of Bhairon Nath and only then would their *darshan* be complete.

Why did I say that after my *darshan* the devotee would have a *darshan* of Bhairon Nath? Some foolish devotees have wondered whether the last deity to be worshipped is also the most exalted and most powerful. Would this mean, they have pondered, that Bhairon Nath was to be more highly revered even than myself especially since it were my own instructions that it would be his *darshan* that would follow my own *darshan* and *only then* would the *darshan* itself be regarded as complete. Some pundits who come here for *darshan* and are very proud of their learning have wondered that perhaps I held Bhairon Nath in such high esteem on account of his great learning and perhaps they too deserve great regard on account of the number of scriptures they have read and memorized.

It is all so stupid! Even had I been willing to deprecate myself in this fashion could it be imagined that I as the Goddess embodying the three energies of the three Supreme Goddesses, Maha Kali, Maha Lakshmi and Maha Saraswati would have thought it fit to deprecate and insult them in this fashion.

The *darshan* is meant to be an instrument for your inner spiritual growth and transformation. You make the fourteen kilometer journey so that you feel yourself that you have made some effort. You are my children and as a mother I would hate to see my children suffer and therefore I am not a believer in self flagellation or torture. However I do not want my children to be indolent or lazy and right effort is needed for spiritual transformation. When you undertake the steep climb to my shrine you exhaust yourself with the effort and you demonstrate to yourself that you are sincere. It is important to undertake the steep climb. Even before you can demonstrate to me that you are sincere, you must demonstrate it to yourself and you prove it to yourself by undertaking this arduous journey. The real *darshan* is given only to him who makes the RIGHT EFFORT.

When Gods and Goddesses create their shrines they do not do so randomly or without thought. We often choose our shrines near the rivers and so you have the many shrines and holy towns that have come up alongside the journey from the mountains through the plains of my beloved spiritual sister, the River Goddess, Ganga Maiya. We also choose our shrines to be at high points in the mountains and so we have Badrinath, Kedarnath and Mount Kailash amongst others.

We have chosen these spots for a particular purpose. When people sit besides besides flowing water they commune with their own spirit. They also commune with their own spirit when they are deep into the mountains and they look down on all creation and see the beauty and vastness of nature for they realize then how petty and trivial so many of their concerns are.

Each shrine has its own spiritual meaning and significance and I do not want to enter into any comparisons here but when you come to my shrine you also visit a shrine that is unique in many ways. It is the shrine of a Goddess that is special because she incorporates within her being three most powerful and divine energies of this universe.

You have come to my shrine and I have designed it such so as to try and make it an instrument of your transformation. It is an example of celestial architecture whose contours you cannot even begin to fathom, but when you depart some of you do feel you have taken with you some of the effects this architecture has on the human soul.

There are pilgrims who go to visit Shrines that are located near Ganga Maiya because they have a dual purpose in mind. To visit the shrine itself and then to have a dip in the holy waters of the river for it has long been said that a dip in the Ganga cleanses you of all sin. Someone is said to have remarked that it is true that when you take a dip in the waters, all the sins immediately leave your body and go and sit on the trees, but when you emerge from the waters, cleansed of all sins, those very same sins that were sitting on the trees come back to sit on you. So what has been achieved?

So what has been achieved? If you have my *darshan* and you feel you have been cleansed of all sins and can now go back to your old life doing exactly what you had been doing before in exactly the same way, what then has been achieved?

And that is why I have decreed that you have Bhairon Nath's *darshan* after my *darshan*. It is because when you start on your *darshan* many of you have qualities that are quite similar to Bhairon Nath. You have knowledge of the scriptures but your conduct is not pure and you can fall a victim to greed and lust anytime.

When you see Bhairon Nath after your *darshan* with me, it is only to show you your own face. You cannot go away anymore thinking that I have had a dip in the Ganges and have come away totally cleansed all ready to begin anew a fresh cycle of misdeeds. You cannot go away with my memory alone for to see Bhairon Nath in the end is to have a close encounter with your own reality.

And then begins the journey of your transformation!

But the human mind is devious. As we, the Gods and Goddesses think of ways and devices by means of which to transform human consciousness so too do you my children think up ways and means of avoiding the transformation, of getting things free, of not doing your assigned tasks, of condemning Bhairon Nath while all the while there is a Bhairon Nath sitting inside you.

But you will protest. I am bad, you will say, but not all that bad. What if I were to tell you that along the journey Bhairon Nath too realized his mistake but thought no penance would suffice. He saw clearly that he had been totally out of his mind and he wished death upon himself. When he continued to follow me through the mountains he no longer came out of disrespect but he came to seek his punishment. It is not true that after his death he sought forgiveness but prior to being beheaded he actually prayed for punishment. He knew of course that if were to be killed by me, he would attain to Heaven but at the time he prayed for punishment he was not propelled by greed of Heaven (as some of you who visit me are) but remorse and a desire to inflict pain on himself to atone for his sin.

WOULD THAT CHANGE YOUR ATTITUDE TOWARDS BHAIRON NATH?

So let me tell you then that this is what truly happened. And I hope you will now not feel that the comparison is unfair. And if it is unfair to some amongst you, do not worry because I am your mother and sometimes I scold you unreasonably, do I not, for some mistake you may not have committed?

Chapter 5

The Merchant

AND THERE WAS A MERCHANT AMONGST
US and the Goddess spake to him thus:

There are many people who come to me because
I am in part a creation of the Goddess Lakshmi- and
yet there is no temple of the Goddess that is as well
known as my shrine is – and so they come to me.
They come to me because I am in part the creation
of the Goddess Lakshmi forgetting that I am in equal
measure the creation of the Goddesses Durga and
Saraswati,

They come to me shouting that my bhandara is
never empty and they shout also that no one returns
empty-handed from the shrine of the Devi.

This is true in some sense but not in the way
many of them think.

There are some who are rich already and who

come to me with the hope that I will make them still richer. They make donations to the temple but all the time they are calculating that the donation may persuade me to grant them unbounded wealth.

They come to me thinking that I am like themselves, for they are themselves easily flattered and so they would try to flatter me by singing my praises from the roof tops. But their praise is not pure for it is a praise with an agenda and the agenda is that listening to them sing my praises I will give them more wealth. They give me a donation and they hope that thereby I will give them unheard of wealth and these are business people whom I do not reward for the money that they give stinks of the bribery that they are used to practice in their daily life. And just as they deny to the reluctant bureaucrat that a bribe is being offered him, so also they would be outraged at any suggestion made by someone that they were offering ME a bribe - but essentially the spirit of their offering is not that different.

How foolish are they who believe that I hold the power to grant limitless wealth and that I ca﹘ he persuaded to distribute this wealth if I am provided with a commission. But, they will say, it is not commission that they give, it is charity and it is a token of their respect and love for me.

Remember this always. Money is immaterial. I do not regard the rich man any higher than the poorest of the poor. For me you are all my children and I do not value those who travel by helicopters to have my *darshan* any more than I value he who trudges up fourteen kilometers on foot. Do not also think that I will value you more because you have come bare footed walking upwards in the heat. It is good if you wish to do so, but do not think that you will earn any merit in doing so. If it is anticipation that by engaging in such labors you will receive special treatment then that special treatment shall certainly not be given. Come to me pure in mind and spirit. Come to me with genuine humility and not the false humility and cunning calculations of politicians and shrewd businessmen. Do your business in the world and earn money through right effort but do not develop the mind of the businessman such that you become someone who is trying to always trying to seek profit, even in spiritual matters. For your businessman's mind will lead you nowhere in the spiritual world, and therefore even from a businessman's point of view it is best that you leave behind your business like mind when you come to me for my *darshan*. Otherwise you will see the sacred pindis but you will not have my *darshan*. And do not try to read my mind, for that you cannot.

If they want to give me something that I will truly appreciate they have to give of themselves.

If you have come to me to seek gain and profit for your business and if you do work rightly I will bless you with further progress. There are also some of my devotees who do come in this spirit and to them I grant my blessing for they earn profit by fair means and the society as a whole benefits from their dealings.

For are not those who come to your shops to buy goods my children any the less and must I not therefore ask of those of you who trade and are business people that your dealings be fair. It is good to make profit and you have every right to make profit, but you do not have the right to cheat other people in the making of that profit. Make profit by all means but do not profiteer from the misery of other people. Employ people to work for you but give them a fair wage and do not try to pay a worker who works for you less than he rightfully deserves, for what you take away from him, I promise I will take away from you. I will take it away sometimes in this life and sometimes in the next, but take away I will. And especially you I will not forget if you have come to my shrine for my blessings and I have granted them and afterwards you have abused the trust I have placed in you. For do not forget that if I am in one way a form of the Goddess Lakshmi, I am also in another way the Goddess Durga incarnate.

Chapter 6

The Aged Man

AND IN THE GROUP, there was an elderly man who could not have been a day less than ninety and people looked at him and remarked on his dedication to undertake such an arduous journey.

And the Goddess spake thus to him:

The ones who come to my shrine are sometimes not even nine months old and sometimes as it is in your case, Bhupathi, they have past the age of ninety.

Yet for me they are all my children. The human being is always emotionally young. You may be a hundred and ten but you may still long to be once more in the presence of your mother. Your earthly mother. But that of course is generally not possible. But it is possible for you to come to me.

People look at Bhupathi and wonder that he has made this pilgrimage on his own at his age. There are no family members accompanying him. A wife may have predeceased him but no accompanying son, daughter, grandson or granddaughter. Why have they not accompanied him? And if he has undertaken this journey alone, is he not to be specially commended?

Bhupathi's wife has predeceased him and his children have deserted him. They are leading their own lives and Bhupathi lives alone in his house, with an old servant who looks after him.

Why has Bhupathi come to me? When elderly people come to me for a *darshan* often they come in the spirit of the trader. It is true that they are more resigned, less energetic and they are not asking me to grant them property, high profits or wealth. They do not come to me with a wish to profit in this world. But why then do I say that they come to me in the spirit of the trader?

It is because they come to me not for profit in this world but for reassurances that they will be comfortable and cared for in the after life or next life whatever you may choose to call it.

They come to me thus as a satrap goes to the Emperor. They come to me confident that I can if I wish arrange things so that they will be comfortable and cared for when they depart from this world. And therefore they come to me essentially in the spirit of the trader.

I cannot be angry with them as I am with the traders. They are old and they are seeking comfort. Is it so wrong to seek comfort in one's old age? I do not feel angry but it is true that I feel sad.

I feel sad for them because their years on this earth have not taught them anything. Their grey hairs only reflect the weariness of their body and the weariness of their spirit. It does not as it should reflect wisdom acquired over the years.

For if they possessed some wisdom they would come to me in a different mode. Even in this mode when they come to me, I will bless them and I will try my best to give them comfort and security in the next life but it will all depend.

If they had come to me in thankfulness and gratitude not making any stated or unstated demands I would have been able to grant them more for would they then have not deserved more? And I, Goddess though I am cannot alter the sacred laws of the universe that to those who deserve I shall give more than to those who deserve less.

There are many mothers on this earth who give more to that child who demands more and a little less to the one who is less demanding. This is human, but I am not human.

Unlike some of your earthly mothers for me the

criteria for giving is not whether you demand it from me, but whether you deserve it. And it is my experience as a Goddess watching over devotees for thousands of years that those who are truly deserving amongst my devotees are those who ask the least.

But they *are* deserving and so they shall receive.

And the ones who demand and do not deserve will find this Mother different from the mother they have encountered in their earthly life, although there too, there are Mothers who do not make demands the criteria for giving.

But Bhupathi is not one of those elderly persons who had made this arduous journey in the hope of a comfortable afterlife with all manner of conveniences.

No, Bhupathi is in a different category. He has come to me to ask for forgiveness. He is convinced that he has committed many sins and he has come to me to seek absolution. The difference between the spirit in which Bhupathi has come and the spirit in which other elderly people have come cannot be overemphasized. They have also come for forgiveness, but there is no inner repentance.

Bhupathi, you are forgiven. Stand up and prostate yourself no more. You are forgiven at once. Do you know why?

It is because you forgive yourself. Each ounce of

repentance brings forth from the divine an equal ounce of forgiveness. I do not mean that you should beat yourself, make wailing sounds or do other kinds of drama to demonstrate your sincerity for in the spiritual world no amount of brilliant acting and histrionics can succeed and when you hit yourself and punish yourself you cast doubts on my ability to see the reality of your repentance. You may be silent from the outside but inside your heart may bleed in penance and I will know this, without any need for you to speak it aloud.

It is not in my power to violate the spiritual laws by granting forgiveness to a sinner who has not truly repented. I want to forgive you, my children but alas you have to merit it first.

And Bhupathi has no thought for what will happen after forgiveness. It is not matter. He does not seek forgiveness IN ORDER THAT HE MAY BE PERMITTED THEREBY TO CROSS AND ENTER THE GATES OF HEAVEN or a benevolent after life. He simply seeks forgiveness. And therefore his repentance is sincere.

You are forgiven this moment, Bhupathi. And if you feel you have not been punished, you are mistaken.

You may feel that your children have abandoned

you for reasons not directly connected with your sins but this is not true for in this strange world of ours everything is interconnected.

Your crimes may have been against someone else, and you may have shown only love to your children and you cannot imagine therefore that they could become the instrument for your punishment for the sins committed by you against others.

But this can happen. And in your case, Bhupathi, it is how it has happened. And although forgiveness is forgiveness and cannot be subdivided for the Mother does not do things by half measure in your case I have to add that it is another reason why the forgiveness you receive is still more complete.

Arise Bhupathi, visit the shrine of Bhairon Nath and go home. And when you reach home you will be surprised to see that your children have returned.

For the Mother does perform miracles but not at random and only when they are deserved.

Chapter 7

The Prostitute

AND THERE WAS A PROSTITUTE in the gathering (which we came to know only just then) and the Goddess looked at her with infinite compassion and said: Speak, my daughter, speak. And then I shall talk to you.

It seemed that the young beautiful girl who stood beside us had been waiting for precisely such a direction for it was as if a tap had been turned on and the words rushed out from her mouth in a torrent. And she spake thus:

'Mother, I have come to you (she sobbed). Mother, I have come to you to you for help. You must help me. You have helped me in the past and I do beseech you to help me once more.

You know, Mother, that I have not had an easy life. My parents died in an accident when I was but a child and I was brought up by my chacha's family.

They were not nice to me at all. I was made to do all the house work, not sent to school and beaten up by my aunt if I made the slightest mistake. My chacha was completely under her influence and would not protect me from her with the result that I took the few clothes I had and one day I caught a train to the nearest big city with a view to somehow find a better life. I escaped from the house, not knowing where to go.

In the big city I knew not where to go and after wandering the streets the whole day, looking for work as a maid servant, I met a young man, who turned out to be a rogue and a rascal. He took me to a place where I was supposed to work as a maid and was promised lodging, food and wages.

The very next day I found that the boy was a pimp and I had been brought to a house of ill repute. I will not say what happened next but you Mother know that I resisted very hard, but there was no other way and before I knew it I had become a prostitute. It was then impossible to go back to my chacha's house.

I have been living this life in the big city for many years now which is not very far from this,

Your Shrine, and your know how much I hate it. I want to escape and do something else with my life. The last time I ran away they found me at the railway station waiting for a train. I was taken back to the house, beaten black and blue and told that should I try to escape again I would be killed.

This time I just climbed on to a bus that was already moving so they could not track me down, and perchance this happened to be a bus full of pilgrims coming to the town below, whence I climbed up to have Your *darshan*.

Yet I know that these people are very nasty and that their threats are real. They have to make an example of me so that no other girl should think of trying to escape from their clutches. They did threaten me on the last occasion that they (the people who were running the brothel) will find me and drag me back to that house of ill repute, and there they will pour acid on me, or set fire to me, or do something so wicked that I cannot but tremble in fear.

Mother, I do not want to go back there, but I know that they are all in league with the police and have already sent my description out for them to be able to trace me out! Mother, I don't want to die! I don't want to go back!! Help me, Mother!!'

And saying this, the girl collapsed on the floor sobbing.

When the girl spake thus, she did not move her lips, but S heard each word clearly. She would not tear out her heart in public and disclose to the world that she was a prostitute but the Mother for her own reasons thought it fit that S (and possibly the others) should hear her words.

And the Mother was silent for a few moments and then she spake thus:

'My Child, It is good that you have come to me.

And it is good that you do not ask me about why in the past certain events happened to you, for there are many who have suffered far less than you have who come to my altar and ask me in anger as to why I being their Mother did not prevent those things happening to them.

What has happened has happened and nothing can change it. There is no need to dwell excessively on it or to ask repeatedly the question: WHY ME?

You have suffered my child but have taken a step away from that life of suffering, and your fate and destiny has carried your footsteps to my Shrine.

And believe me that no harm will come to you now that you are at the Mother's altar.

You will be protected but not in the way you think. I will make no apparition to confront and cut off the heads of the monsters who seek to make your life hell.

You will be protected if you are ready to receive my blessings and if you are ready for me to help and protect you.

There are many who come here for my blessings and they go away not empty handed (for there is a Gift for each one of you) but certainly without my blessings for while I am their Mother if what they ask of me is unholy or impure I do not bless them in their endeavors.

But there are still others who come to me for my blessings and they too go away without my blessings but that is not because I did not bless them but rather that they chose not to understand or accept my blessing and to see that although blessings can be free, oftentimes a blessing comes only to him who had prepared himself to receive it. And they cannot say that I did not tell them what to do in order to receive the blessing, for if you stand at my altar in silence and in prayer I will come to you and you will know what it is that I expect from you.

And so to you, dear daughter, I do bless you now. And I do hope that you will do what you need to do to receive my blessing and to make it work for you.

And you have prostrated yourself before me, and while you have sobbed and cried in your sorrow, you have yet not been so utterly absorbed in your own distress that you have been unable to hear my words.

For have you not come here to hear me speak? And I have spoken and you have understood.

You have understood my darling daughter, that you are blessed. And you have readied yourself to receive the blessing.

AND WHAT IS THIS READINESS THAT I SPEAK OF?

The readiness to allow me to enter you!

For I will not stand aside and appear as an apparition in this instance, but I shall be within you and I shall be *you*, and if you believe this, if you truly keep faith with me, Your Mother, then no harm can come to you!

You will have my sword that is made of a steel that has not been seen in this earthly life and it will have a razor like sharpness that can not only cut through the human flesh of your enemies but it can sunder and cast aside any living, natural, unnatural and supernatural force that dares to confront with you.

So go my child and fear no more. You have been blessed by the Mother herself and her protection will follow you wherever you go.'

And S saw to his amazement that the woman who had lain crying and sobbing on the mud floor but a few moments ago, suddenly stiffened her body and when she rose her eyes were clear and no longer dimmed by her tears. And with those clear eyes she gazed upon the Devi with respect, love and adoration and it seemed to S that the Devi then looked back upon herself as she gazed upon the young girl.

Chapter 8

The Childless Couple

AND THERE WAS A CHILDLESS COUPLE who stood there who seemed married for some years and their expression was one of sadness as they stood before the Devi, their hands folded in prayer.

And it seemed that this couple was childless though they had been married for some years and had come the Goddess to ask for the boon of a child for the Goddess when she spoke to them, spake thus:

YOU HAVE COME TO ME to seek my blessings that you may have the boon of a child. And many before you have come to me asking for a similar boon and some of those who have stood here and prayed have been blessed with a child soon after they have visited my shrine.

And they have been delighted and have attributed it to my powers for they were childless for many years and now suddenly within a few months of my *darshan* the woman is carrying a child. And when they attribute it to my powers they are not wrong in this but many amongst them do not realize that my powers too have to work through them and if they are not ready and deserving that I too can do little.

There are couples who have come here and prayed for the gift of a male child and this is because of the prestige and status given in some places to the parents of a son and it is also because it is believed that the son extends the lineage of the family whereas the daughter does not, and to those who come in this fashion or manner I withhold all manner of favor or blessing for they are so ignorant as to not realize that the Mother to whom they have come for their blessings was herself once a girl on this earth, and they do thereby disrespect her and seek something which cannot be granted. It is not unnatural to have a preference for a boy or girl and I do not judge any preference based on a natural affection but when the affection is not natural but influenced by unhealthy, impure and unholy thoughts of status and prestige then the parents are not deserving of any blessing and especially not from the Mother at whose altar they pretend to pray. For such prayers are mere pretences to prayer and as they lack real sincerity cannot be granted.

And those who come to my altar and pray in this fashion do not realize that the Divine does not make difference between girl and boy and the daughter is equally precious as any son may be. And the Mother will not be an instrument by which you can perpetuate ideas that need to be discarded for if you are granted a son he would become an instrument for the perpetuation of these very ideas.

You stand together and have folded your hands in prayer as you gaze at my statues and I do not doubt your devotion or sincerity but I ask you if you also look at each other with the respect that a husband should have for his wife, or a wife for her husband.

For this child that you wish to have should be a symbol of the love and affection in which you regard each other and although the child is coming from the future that you know nothing of, yet it is influenced by the relationship between the parents.

And are you seeking a child that shall be a symbol of your love as man and woman or are you seeking a child to satisfy the wishes of your parents, the wishes of your relatives and to silence their questioning?

And do you want a child who shall be a living witness to your love as husband and wife or do you seek a child that shall fulfill your unattained ambitions for if you seek the latter you have already prepared a strait jacket into which your child shall not fit even before he has been born. And no child can fit into the strait jacket of the ambitions of his parents.

And do you want a child so that you can give it your unflagging and unconditional love, the same love which you claim and get from me, or do you seek a child so that it can look after you in your old age and perform your last rites, for if these are the reasons that are uppermost in your mind when you ask for a child you are not deserving of the most pure and sacred gift from the Divine.

There are couples who have come here and stood and prayed and they have been blessed. Their pilgrimage to my shrine has dissolved all the mutual recriminations that they might have held against each other. The husband who blamed his wife for not bearing him a child and the woman who felt blamed for not bearing a child are not fitting receptacles for any gift that I may chose to grant them, for while they have come to the Mother and the bhandar of the Mother is ever plentiful and does not grudge even those little deserving a gift, a Child is the most precious gift that existence has to offer and it cannot be given by me to those who stand at my altar in a spirit of mutual recrimination and hostility.

You will be ready to receive my blessings if you have allowed this pilgrimage to purify you to the extent that you have dissolved all acrimony and look at each other with deep respect that is a reflection of the higher respect and devotion that you show me.

You will receive my blessings if you seek to bestow on the child unconditional love and not have uppermost in your mind the idea that this child shall look after you in your old age or carry out your last rites, though that may well follow naturally.

You will have my blessings if you ask with pure mind and spirit and you shall have more than my blessings for you for the child that comes shall also be blessed.

And such are the mysteries of this existence that the child who has been blessed in this fashion even before its birth has a special purity to it, and this is the case even though all children are Divine and Divinity cannot be measured, divided or multiplied.

Chapter 9

The Scientist

AND THERE WAS A VERY WELL DRESSED AND DIGNIFIED LOOKING GENTLEMAN who stood in the gathering and as he stood there with his hands folded in prayer, the Devi addressed him and to him, she spake thus:

THERE ARE SOME AMONGST YOU who live decent responsible lives and you who stand there in respectful silence are one such being. I cannot say that you believe in me, but nevertheless you have made the pilgrimage and do stand in front of me with your hands folded. And you do not stand in any hypocritical fashion but you stand with a measure of doubt and it is therefore that I say that you do not truly believe in me.

And I do not say that this is anything wrong or that those who not believe absolutely or those who believe but with doubt, or even those who absolutely do not believe in me are any less worthy than those of my children who believe and trust in me.

For to the Mother, or at least to this Mother, all her children are equally beloved whether they trust and believe in her or not.

And you have come to me because although you have been a respected scientist all your life towards the evening of your life you have seen and known enough to realize the limits of science and rationality.

You now sense that in your youth and middle age you did not have a proper appreciation for the mysteries of this life, but your life's experiences have now taught you that there is something beyond the rational which is the supra rational and that possibly there is something still beyond that and that something is embodied in me.

And that is why you, a scientist, a man given to logic and rationality have come to me at this stage in your life. You have come to me, but you carry forward with you a doubt which has come from your training as a scientist and a lifetime of questioning and skepticism.

And I do not in truth feel troubled by this doubt

that you have in your mind for in a way this is a sign of health and maturity. I say in a way because while it is good to doubt, it is also good to trust.

Keep your doubt in the market place for you need it there because it is full of people who wish to make your money theirs and who would not think twice about cheating you to make their own profit.

But when you have come to your Mother let your emotions flow for once for you have spent a life time acting as a watchman and a guard not allowing your emotions to spill over. That was good policy in the laboratory and it made sound sense in the market place but you have been overcautious with your wife and even your children, and now that you have somehow managed to quell your doubts to the extent that you have come here to the shrine of the Mother, see if you can cast aside all your doubts and skepticism for there is much that I wish to give to you but you have to be ready to receive it.

I say I welcome your doubts because in truth doubt is necessary not only for the scientists who wish to uncover the truths nature has hidden in her bosom but doubt is necessary even in matters of the heart and spirit.

Doubt is necessary but only till you reach the stage where you can cast aside your doubts, and that stage, my child, is not at the point where to take the example of science you have finally uncovered some great scientific principle or law of nature but in matters of the heart and spirit you have to cast the doubt a little ahead of reaching that point.

When you come to me, you will have to cast aside your doubts before the truth is revealed to you, for this is not science and these are not scientific principles that will be revealed to you here, but the truth about the scientist himself, his inner being and this is a far far higher truth that the truth of the scientific principles that you have uncovered and seek to discover more of.

IN SCIENCE, YOU CAST ASIDE YOUR DOUBTS when the truth is revealed to you. The truth is revealed and your doubts disappear simultaneously, but here there is a gap between the time you lose your doubts and when possibly the truth will be revealed to you.

And in truth if you search your heart you will find that when you stand thus before me, your heart is begging you to cast aside your doubts and to let your emotions flow.

Listen to your heart, if you can. The little voice inside you is telling you not to doubt any more. It is telling you that while you may have been right in doubting till this very moment in your life, finally, oh finally, you have come to the place where you can cast aside your doubts completely even though the truth has not been revealed to you.

A child begins his life in trust and then slowly slowly bit by bit the world outside teaches him not to trust but to doubt. The heart was flowing but the mind was not yet mature and therefore it had no weapons with which to argue against those who told it not to flow. The mind was too weak to resist and then the heart was suppressed and the mind began to strengthen itself.

And the mind became stronger and stronger until a point was reached where the heart was left far behind and the person forgot the time when his heart was flowing and was held back because the mind was then too weak to argue against stronger minds that told him to keep his feelings in check.

You are your heart and also your mind but during your first years on this earth it was your heart that was the stronger of the two and then as you grew in years the mind picked up because the world could not allow the free flowing undisciplined heart that had no mind to keep it in check. And then the mind became stronger and stronger and a point was reached when it left the heart far behind and forgot that the first taste of true and pure happiness is found with the heart and the pleasures of the mind and the body lack that spark or touch of divinity if they are experienced in separation from the heart.

The child learns to harden his heart and learns not to trust and then when the mind begins to develop it is told that it must move with caution, with skepticism and with doubt.

And therefore my child I tell you who have spent a life time in the pursuit of science with the assistance of the doubting questioning mind that while doubts are necessary for the proper investigation of the universe that exists without or outside you, doubts must be surrendered for an apprehension of the universe inside you.

The outside universe is investigated and truths are discovered but those so called truths are actually merely hypotheses and are relativistic in nature and that is why you find that the truth was revealed and the doubts disappeared.

In reality a hypothesis was revealed and your doubts disappeared. No truth was actually revealed and you may discover decades later that you were mistaken to have surrendered your doubts.

And here the exact reverse will happen for you will surrender your doubts and then the truth will be revealed to you, but this truth is the essential truth and is not a mere hypothesis or relativistic in nature.

But, you will ask me, Mother why should I surrender my doubts when they have worked so well for me till now and when it was my first major childhood lesson to learn not to trust, not to trust strangers, not to trust that others will always be good, that elders will always keep their promises, that good will be rewarded and evil punished and so on and forth endlessly.

You must surrender your doubt because till you do so, you cannot be transformed. Why do you cling to these doubts? In the outside world there were those who wished to cheat you and you did not trust them out of a fear, but you do not fear that I will cheat you and still you do not let go of your doubts.

You do not fear that I will cheat you but you fear that your mind will somehow weaken, this mind that you hold in such high regard, but which bereft from contact with the heart can never make you have even a taste of the higher pleasure or ecstasy that contact with the divine brings.

Do not fear that your mind will weaken. This is the original fear in you for your heart was wounded when it did not have a mind that could protect it. It is good to have a strong mind, but the strength of your mind should not become an obstacle and your mind should be strong yet supple enough to step out of the way when it is not needed.

You are not the mind, you need to know, but alas this truth will be revealed to you only if you dissipate your doubts and allow your feelings to flow.'

And the Scientist stood there and it seemed that something was about to happen for his body suddenly shook, but it was momentary and he soon reassumed his earlier devotional posture.

And he had the *darshan* but he was not yet ready on this occasion for the ultimate blessing that the Mother sought to shower on him.

Chapter 10

The Artist

AND THERE WAS A LEAN UNSHAVEN MAN in his early thirties in the group, and this man carried with him a jhola or cloth bag and from this he withdrew a sketch pad and at the beginning of the *darshan* he seemed to draw something on it briefly before replacing it in the handbag.

And this man was an Artist and the Goddess seemed to gaze upon him for long and then she spake thus:

'I see you, my son, and I look at you for long for you are an artist and artists and poets, are often seekers of beauty and they are especially close to me for this reason.

But I look at you thus because when you seek out beauty you are in a way not alone because each person in this cave at the moment and all persons in the world in fact seek out something akin to beauty and that is refinement which is in one way just another name for beauty but it need not be beauty as understood by the artist, the painter and the poet.

What is this refinement? It is surely a quality that is found where beauty is to be found but it is far more subjective in nature for most people will agree what is meant by beauty but what I mean by refinement here is totally subjective and without morality.

What then is this refinement that can even be immoral?

It is a quality in the world that is akin to beauty and all mankind searches for it, but each person sees it according to his or her own understanding of it.

You will find it in the forest when all is suddenly hush, you will find it in the music of the birds, you will find it in beautiful sunrises and sunsets and you will find it in the starry nights.

But you will exclaim that this is beauty!

Yes, so it is, but this quality you will find also in what is ugly or what may appear ugly.

You may find a gastronome's appetite ugly for instance. He may be feasting on animal flesh that is a product of violence but yet I say to you that there may be in the savoring of that food an element that he seeks: that of refinement. The wine drinker seeks that refinement and so does the alcoholic and so even the user of drugs.

The Goddess does not tell you to devour animal flesh or to take drink and swallow drugs. Far from it!

Would that you needed no such pleasures for they are transient and shallow and yet I say to you that you may experience some refinement even there and what I tell you today is that taste is the taste of the essential and of the beyond.

Refinement is experienced at the higher levels of all or most pleasurable experience and it may be that to have the experience of that pleasure some one has caused suffering but yet at the highest levels of that pleasure you will have that glimpse of the beyond only you may not realize that this is what it is.

And if the gastronome, the alcoholic and the drug user would but savor that refinement for a moment he would realize that it he wishes to extend that moment and not lose it forever he has to cast aside flesh prepared for devouring and throw away the wine bottles and the drugs for those are necessary conditions for the sustained enjoyment of the refinement which they had barely glimpsed and it was gone.

But you will say, surely lust cannot be refined, and I will say to you, my child, that even lust has its refined dimensions. Your physical relationship with another human being can give you at the moment of ecstasy a taste of utter refinement which is another word for a glimpse of the beyond.

You will think it over and perhaps you will accept that this can be the case with great lovers but surely there can be no refinement in acts of violence. And I will say to you that doubtless it is unlikely but not impossible for even in rendering acts of violence refinement is possible for do not forget that when I take the form of Durga or Kali I do then commit violence but it is a violence that is refined and exalted and the person is blessed upon whom such violence may befall.

But you will cry out this is SO UNFAIR. Why should divine grace touch acts of immorality and it would perhaps be a consolation for you if I said that it does not but the truth is that there are people who are sick who cause suffering to others and you might think that they are not deserving enough to be blessed with a vision of the beyond but yet I will tell you that in the haze which surrounds the alcoholic, the drug addict and those addicted to the pleasures of the flesh there comes a moment when the divine penetrates and it has at that moment the potential to alter their state of consciousness.

But, you will cry out, Mother surely these things are most condemnable and a term such as refinement cannot be used for such dastardly, inhuman and cowardly acts.

And I say to you that in the subjectivity of the person who does what is so evidently wrong and immoral there is yet a refinement, an appreciation of beauty.

And it is thus that I say to you that all men seek refinement.

As an artist when you seek beauty you are close to me for you seek either pure beauty which is utterly refined or you seek a combination of refinement with goodness but you also sometimes do seek a combination of refinement with evil.

But you will say you are not that but you seek only to depict it.

And it is true that in much of what you draw or paint as an artist you show what is ugly or repulsive in the world but you show even that with refinement and here I speak not of you as an individual artist but as an artist epitomizing all artists in the world

For there is an aesthetics even in depicting what is ugly.

And when you throw your vomit on to the canvas you take care to refine it but you suppose that you are separate from it and indeed in a sense you are separate for you are not directly a creator of that ugliness but perhaps even in order to depict it well you need to be a small participant.

And so I say to you that therefore within the subjectivity of those who do what are commonly understood to be sinful acts there can also be found a refinement and when I say this I do not mean to condone their actions in any way but merely to point out to you that man cannot ultimately even at his most evil be separated from his essential humanity.

And it is this essential humanity that makes him and all men seekers of refinement. And somewhere in their searching they do seek also the ultimate refinement

All men seek that refinement but almost all with few exceptions seek it in the wrong places and here I mean to include those who seek it in nature or in actions both good and bad.

And the refinement that they seek, when they have even but a taste of it, they have at that time a taste of the essential and it does not then matter that they do good or bad.

And when Artists come and stand before me they do stand in all humility, be they painters, singers, musicians, sculptors or other manner of creators for they are standing before the one who paints on the ultimate canvas, and all creation is at once a canvas and a painting and a song and a dance and what the Artist does is merely to imitate and to try and transmit to others a taste of that higher refinement that he has felt in his being.

The Artist stands before me in all humility but amongst his peers and other Non Artists he shows temperament and the reason for this is that he has had glimpses of excellence and refinement and he seeks to protect anyone from throwing dirt on it by showing temperament. This is what he tells himself but in truth he massages his ego that he has glimpsed or known for a moment a taste of ultimate refinement. And he thinks that he is therefore someone special.

And I say to you, Artist, who stand before me that if you truly desire to come close to me, you will have to cast aside the ego and become a pure passage for the beyond. You will have to throw out this temperament for although you tell yourself it protects your art from assault, it acts as a stumbling block on your spiritual as well as artistic advancement, for the two cannot be separated and it is true that as Art reaches higher levels it leaves the lower morality behind and at the very highest levels Art touches the feet of the Divine

Chapter 11

The Seeker

AND THERE WAS A BEARDED MIDDLE AGED MAN in the group, a man who had traveled tó many different parts of the world over the years, and this person was always polite and courteous but did not mix much with the others and he was a Seeker and to him to Goddess spake thus:

'There are many who come to me, and most of them come because they are troubled with issues in their earthly life, but some of the devotees come to me because they seek a higher truth.

These are the Seekers. And you, who have traveled far and wide and have been exposed to many different cultures in the world, are one of those.

But you are rare even among the Seekers who come to me for there are different kinds of Seekers.

The most common kind of Seeker is one who joined hands with Goodness early on in their life, but while they joined hands with Goodness they were, unbeknown to themselves also simultaneously attracted to the darker forces of human nature.

It is difficult to be good in this world.

And the reason is that when early on a child who has been taught to be good by his mother, practices this advice he finds that there are no immediate earthly rewards to his acts of goodness

And when early on in his life a child sees how injustice often prevails in the world and how people get away with wrong actions he is torn between the gratification that wrong actions often bring and the punishment that good deeds entail.

For good deeds often entail a sacrifice and the sacrifice becomes to the child a kind of punishment. Not only is he not rewarded for his goodness but he is punished for it is a kind of sacrifice.

And therefore while he has chosen to align himself with the forces of good, there is a questioning in his mind as to why this should happen.

It is but a test, he tells himself. The rewards will perhaps follow a bit later. And his parent reassures him that is indeed the case and he will be rewarded for all the good deeds that he did in the afterlife and those who acted wrongly will be punished in the afterlife.

And reassured thus, he continues with his good deeds.

But the afterlife is often not sufficient compensation for him, for even though he trusts in it, yet a small voice tells him, who knows whether in fact an afterlife exists at all?

And he wants immediate gratification of a kind, any kind and therefore he creates a gratification and that gratification is the massaging of his ego, that he has done good, and Gods and Goddesses are aware of his goodness, and he is especially beloved of them and he himself will have a special place beside the Mother Goddess as a saint.

And this remains the most common psychology of many of the Seekers who come to me.

And many of these Seekers come to me late in their lives. They believe that they have lead good lives, and indeed in a sense they have, but now in the late afternoon or evening of their lives they begin to wonder whether they have done enough good and also as to whether their thinking has been right that they will be rewarded and they then come to the

Mother for further reassurance and comfort.

And they are Seekers it is true and it is also true many of them have been Good in a way.

I say that they have been Good in a way because their Goodness is not of the highest purity for they have also wedded themselves to the darker forces in existence.

And what are these darker forces and why is their Good not pure enough?

The darker forces are their very belief that they will be rewarded in heaven for the good deeds that they have done on this earth. The darker force is their overdeveloped ego which they have pampered and nourished by telling themselves over and over again that THEY are good and especially close to me. And finally the darker force they are aligned with is the hatred and anger that they fling upon those who do wrong, and the satisfaction that they derive from imagining the punishments that will be rendered to those who are wrong doers in their eyes.

And this renders their goodness impure and far from being given a seat as a Saint sitting beside me they separate and distance themselves by their own acts and expectations.

And this is my message for those Seekers.

Do good but do not make a sacrifice of it.

Sometimes it may be better not to do good if it becomes a burden on your soul, for otherwise you may seek nourishment by massaging your ego and that good will no longer remain good for it will have been poisoned by your motives.

Do good but keep no expectations of reward from your actions other than the feeling of happiness that a good deed brings to you.

Do good but do not condemn those others who do not act as you do for the world is a free place and it will be tyranny to force everyone to do a predetermined good under compulsion.

And are you an authority on what is good? For if you imagine yourself to be an authority you are not good but merely a tyrant for while good is oftentimes apparent, sometimes you have to see things very carefully and minutely before you can come to any conclusion on what will be good. And those who imagine themselves to be authorities on goodness are in truth often ego massagers who love to dictate and dominate.

And there are these kind of Seekers who come to

me and imagine themselves to be especially favored by me but I draw no distinction between such Seekers and those who come with simple demands in a humble non assuming way. And if truth were to be told I often feel these simpler people asking for simple gratifications to be closer to me than those who beat the drums loudly in my name.

But as I said to you, Seeker, there are many kinds of Seekers and you belong to the rare category of seekers who do good but seek no reward for it in heaven. Perhaps you do less good than others but what you do you do with a purity that is missing from those who loudly proclaim themselves to be my disciples.

And you have kept aloof from the others for this reason only because you seek not to join a club of mutually admiring devotees who congratulate each other every day on their spiritual progress.

You are a rare seeker but what you miss is depth of vision and insight.

And that vision and insight will come to you by and by.

Perhaps not today, not tomorrow, but the day after...

And you are a Seeker and perhaps you need to

seek some more.'

And with this the Goddess gave a smile and was silent.

The Seeker too was silent but he was accepting of the Devi's directions for he came with little demands as befitted a true Seeker.

And perhaps, one day, not so far ahead, he thought, he would have an apprehension of a higher truth. But he thought this without any expectation.

Chapter 12

The Gift

AND THEN THE MOTHER LOOKED AT ALL OF US gathered together in that small cave and spake thus to us:

'In the beginning I spoke to all of you, my children, and told you about myself and the meaning behind some of my symbols and legends, and then I spoke to each of you individually, and now when it is time for you to all depart – till you come again – let me give you something which you can take with you. This will be my gift to you and it is one that you can use for the rest of your life.

A gift is something you get whether you deserve it or not. In fact when I give a gift it does not matter that you deserve it.

Do I not shower my love and affection on you

unconditionally and you too must bring to your love that purity that you shower it to those around you without any condition or expectation of return.

You have come here to my shrine with the knowledge that the Mother will put no conditions and will shower you with her love and indeed it is so;

But do you not see that the world is starved of love because you are all holding back your love till you feel you have found somebody who deserves.

Do not be hoarders, keeping back your love but rather spend it all and you will find that more is coming, and you will find that your love is returned. It is strange but true that when you drop all expectations of it being returned that you find that it is being returned after all.

And do not become judges about whether so and so person is deserving of your affection, for as you judge so shall you be judged and if you judge in this fashion then you are already judged by the Almighty as being rather poor in spirit and lacking generosity.

For has existence held back its sunshine for you

to enjoy. Does the wind refuse to caress your hair because you have not been a good child? And does the rain not fall cooling the parched earth without any thought of whether it is deserved.

But you will say, Mother, I was generous in giving love and I found that I was betrayed, and I will say to you that you can be betrayed only if you already had an expectation of a return when you gave your love.

And if it happens such that the person to whom you give your love insults or abuses you, then turn away if you must, but turn away not in anger but in sorrow that the person could not understand you.

But bear in mind that you do not have a right that all persons understand you for if there was perfect communication between human beings it would be a simple negation to the world that we know and a meaningless impossibility.

Turn away in sorrow and with an inner smile forgive and forget it all for you do not have the right that the person on whom you shower love, either return that love, or understand that love or even accept that love.

And if he does any of these three things, you are the one who has to be grateful.

For when you love, ostensibly you are giving a Gift to the other but truly speaking you are also giving to yourself, for the very act of loving gives a shine to your personality and adds a divine grace to your being that cannot be purchased anywhere in this man made world where everything has a price but nothing has true value.

I have showered upon you my unconditional love and I see from the sudden freshness in your being after the tired journey to my shrine that you have received it,

And today right now I will give to you my Gift'

And here the Mother finished speaking and then she put her hand forward and something happened.

There was a blazing flash of light and then suddenly S saw that there was whiteness all around.

It was a white light but unlike any he had ever seen for normally white light means that there is an absence of color but this white light was different.

It seemed to contain everything and it was not an absence but a presence.

He felt a delight he had never known before. It was similar to a dream which he had had many years ago where in his fantasy he had visited an exotic sun kissed beach but this was such a beautiful feeling that he was at a loss to think of anything in his past that remotely resembled such happiness.

When a painter looks at a canvas he thinks of the colors he can fill it up with and so too when a sculptor seeks a block of marble a vision comes to him of what the figurines that the block of marble is hiding, but that is an empty, desolate and dry whiteness whereas the whiteness that S now beheld was full of meaning and life. It was a whiteness of sound in which he could hear all the beautiful music he had ever heard in his life and the music he had not even heard. It was a whiteness of vision in which he saw more beautiful sunsets that he had ever seen and it seemed to contain within its body marvelous sights and colors that he had not known existed. He saw the Goddess too in a final beautiful vision and then she disappeared....

He had known that the heart could sing but that the heart could itself become a flute and the music and the musician could become one was a unique and unforgettable experience. His heart was singing as it had sung in the past when he had been with his beloved and this time there was no beloved but yet his heart sang and it sang more deeply and profoundly for that.

And then he seemed to awaken from a sleep and he was in the cave before the three pindis representing the Goddess, and there were the others with him inside the cave and from their expression he could not make out whether they had witnessed what he had seen.

And he was told by someone that he would have to step forward and so he continued in a barely sentient fashion.

For the vision he had sought had appeared before him by Her Grace but then it had vanished.

And when he was out of the cave he collapsed and appeared to lose consciousness and when he awoke he remembered everything clearly but could not see any of the others who had been in the cave beside him receiving the *darshan* from the Goddess. And when he searched for them in the hotels and caravanserai outside the shrine he could not find any of them and when he described their appearance individually too, no one could tell him that such a person had been seen by them. Not the aged man, nor the merchant, nor the childless couple and nor even the prostitute whose beauty would have made her stand out in a crowd.

And then he gave up searching and wondered if perhaps the whole thing had been a vision but when he searched in his pockets he found a white flower.

It was the self same flower that the Goddess had given to each of them at the very beginning of the Darshan and it was white and delicate and fresh as if it had only just been plucked.

He kept the flower with him as a reminder of the grace and love which the Goddess had showered on him and when the flower died he bought a blank diary from the stationary which had nothing written on it and he kept it inside the diary and everyday for the rest of his life he would gaze at the white pages of the diary, turn to the flower and then look back at the whiteness.

When S thought of how he would explain the vision to others he thought he would need to write about it in a book and that he would leave a blank page of whiteness to show others what was present in whiteness if one could only see it. And there was no other way in truth to demonstrate what he had just witnessed.